ROSETTA

VOYAGE TO A COMET

By John Hamilton

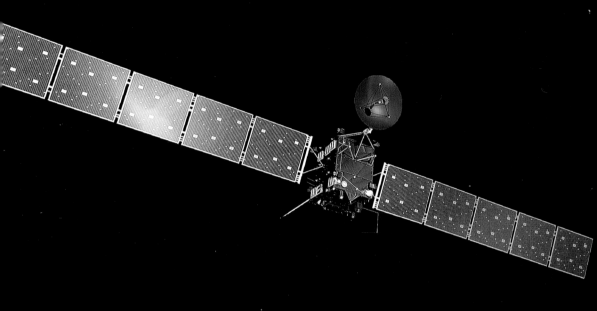

XTREME SPACECRAFT

A&D Xtreme
An imprint of Abdo Publishing | abdopublishing.com

abdopublishing.com

Published by Abdo Publishing, a division of ABDO, PO Box 398166, Minneapolis, Minnesota
55439. Copyright ©2018 by Abdo Consulting Group, Inc. International copyrights reserved in
all countries. No part of this book may be reproduced in any form without written permission
from the publisher. A&D Xtreme™ is a trademark and logo of Abdo Publishing.

Printed in the United States of America, North Mankato, MN.
052017
052017

Editor: Sue Hamilton
Graphic Design: Sue Hamilton
Cover Design: Candice Keimig
Cover Photo: iStock
Interior Photos: All photos European Space Agency or NASA.

Websites
To learn more about Xtreme Spacecraft, visit abdobooklinks.com. These links are routinely
monitored and updated to provide the most current information available.

Publisher's Cataloging-in-Publication Data

Names: Hamilton, John, author.
Title: Rosetta: voyage to a comet / by John Hamilton.
Other titles: Voyage to a comet
Description: Minneapolis, MN : Abdo Publishing, 2018. | Series: Xtreme
    spacecraft | Includes index.
Identifiers: LCCN 2016962230 | ISBN 9781532110139 (lib. bdg.) |
    ISBN 9781680787986 (ebook)
Subjects: LCSH: Space flight--Juvenile literature. | Interplanetary voyages--
    Juvenile literature. | Outer space--Exploration--Juvenile literature.
Classification: DDC 523.6--dc23
LC record available at http://lccn.loc.gov/2016962230

CONTENTS

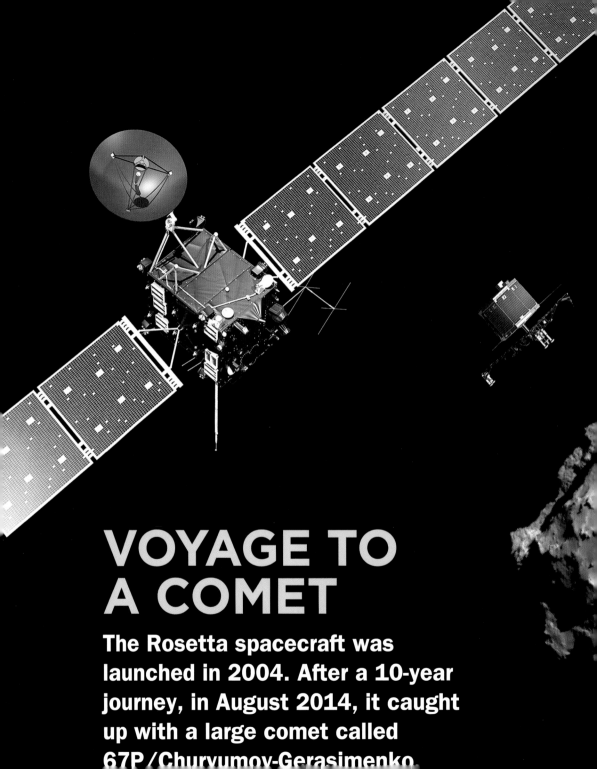

VOYAGE TO A COMET

The Rosetta spacecraft was launched in 2004. After a 10-year journey, in August 2014, it caught up with a large comet called 67P/Churyumov-Gerasimenko.

It was the first time in history that a spacecraft intercepted a comet and followed it partway around the Sun. It was also the first time a remote probe landed on a comet's surface. Rosetta's history-making mission is helping scientists better understand comets, and the birth of our solar system.

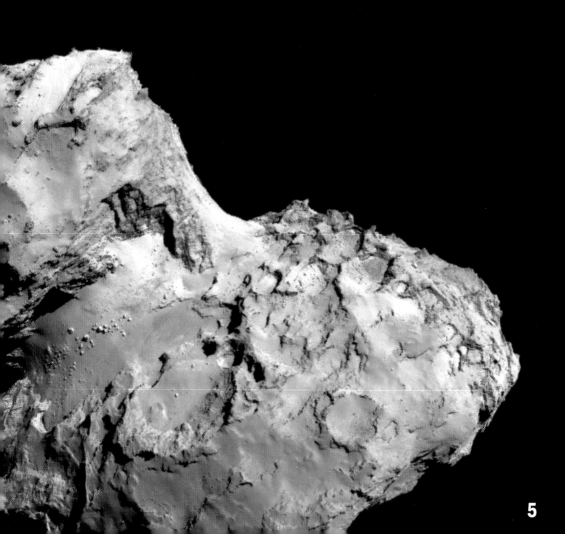

WHY GO TO A COMET?

People have been amazed by comets since ancient times. These mysterious lights in the night sky, with their spectacular, glowing tails, were once thought to predict death and disaster. Today, we know comets are large hunks of ice, dust, and rocks speeding through space.

Halley's comet streaks across the sky in 1986. The well-known comet is visible from Earth every 75 to 76 years. It will next appear in 2061.

A close-up view of the center, or nucleus, of Halley's comet taken on March 13, 1986, by the European Space Agency's Giotto spacecraft.

Many comets travel around the Sun in large, elliptical orbits. They regularly return, sometimes hundreds of years later. Others speed past the Sun once, never to be seen again.

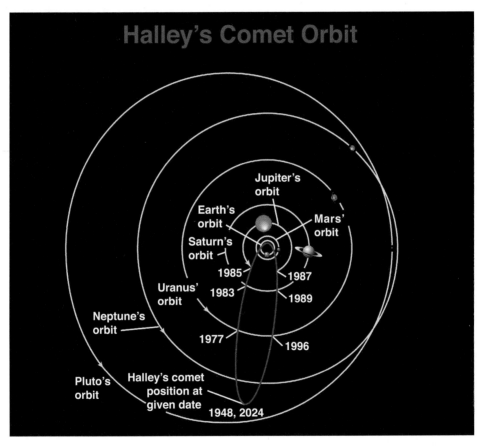

Halley's Comet Orbit

Jupiter's orbit

Earth's orbit

Mars' orbit

Saturn's orbit

1985

1987

Uranus' orbit

1983

1989

Neptune's orbit

1977

1996

Pluto's orbit

Halley's comet position at given date

1948, 2024

 XTREME FACT – In the 1500s, Danish astronomer Tycho Brahe disproved the idea that comets were part of Earth's atmosphere. Instead, Brahe proved that comets came from far away, much farther than the Moon.

Most comets come from the Kuiper belt or the Oort Cloud. They are regions of icy debris far beyond the planet Neptune's orbit. Astronomers estimate there may be one trillion comets or more in these faraway regions. Billions of years ago, many comets crashed into Earth. Perhaps they brought water and the chemical building blocks of life

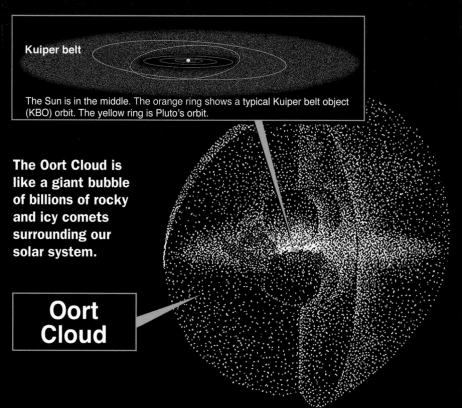

Kuiper belt

The Sun is in the middle. The orange ring shows a typical Kuiper belt object (KBO) orbit. The yellow ring is Pluto's orbit.

The Oort Cloud is like a giant bubble of billions of rocky and icy comets surrounding our solar system.

Oort Cloud

Studying comets is like opening a time capsule. They may give us clues about how the early solar system formed, and how life began on Earth.

Scientists closely studied the flyby of comet Siding Spring with Mars in 2014. The comet came within 87,000 miles (140,000 km) of the Red Planet.

 XTREME FACT – Astronomers believe most comets formed at the same time as the outer planets of our solar system, about 4.6 billion years ago.

PAST MISSIONS

In 1986, spacecraft from several countries studied Halley's comet as it made its closest approach to the Sun.

Halley's Comet 1986

XTREME FACT – Halley's comet is named after English astronomer Edmond Halley. In the early 1700s, he discovered that many comets return regularly. He predicted one comet would return every 76 years. That comet became known as Halley's comet.

In 2001, NASA's Deep Space 1 spacecraft took very detailed photos of comet 19P/Borrelly.

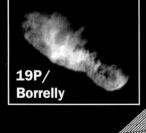

19P/Borrelly

81P/Wild

In 2004, NASA's Stardust spacecraft collected dust particles from comet 81P/Wild. It returned the samples to Earth in 2006.

In 2005, a probe from NASA's Deep Impact spacecraft collided with comet 9P/Tempel. The crater gave Deep Impact a glimpse of the comet's interior. It contained less ice than expected.

9P/Tempel

PLANNING AND BUILDING

The Rosetta spacecraft was built by the European Space Agency (ESA). NASA contributed some scientific instruments. Rosetta was shaped like a box, about 7 feet (2 m) wide. The spacecraft's mission was to explore comet 67P/Churyumov-Gerasimenko.

ESA scientists perform tests on Rosetta at the European Space Research and Technology Centre (ESTEC) in Noordwijk, the Netherlands.

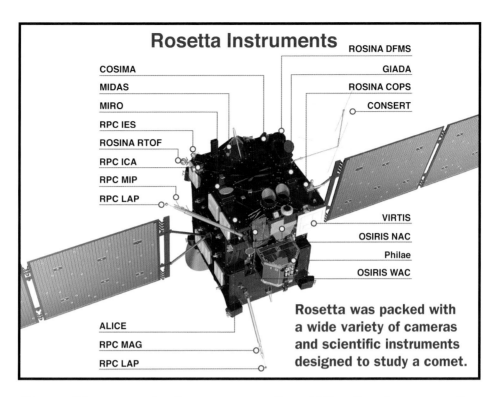

Rosetta Instruments

COSIMA
MIDAS
MIRO
RPC IES
ROSINA RTOF
RPC ICA
RPC MIP
RPC LAP

ROSINA DFMS
GIADA
ROSINA COPS
CONSERT

VIRTIS
OSIRIS NAC
Philae
OSIRIS WAC

ALICE
RPC MAG
RPC LAP

Rosetta was packed with a wide variety of cameras and scientific instruments designed to study a comet.

Rosetta carried many scientific instruments. They were designed to analyze the comet's rocks, ice, and gasses. Rosetta's electrical power came from two large solar arrays. Rosetta also carried a probe called Philae (fee-lay). Its mission was to land on the comet and send back pictures and data.

XTREME FACT – The Rosetta spacecraft is named after the Rosetta Stone. The Philae lander gets its name from the Philae Obelisk. Both of these artifacts helped us translate ancient Egyptian picture-words called hieroglyphs. Astronomers hope that Rosetta and Philae will help us understand our solar system.

LAUNCH

Rosetta left Earth on March 2, 2004. It blasted off from the European Space Agency's Guiana Space Centre. The launch center is in French Guiana, South America.

Rosetta is loaded into the rocket at the Guiana Space Centre on February 18, 2004.

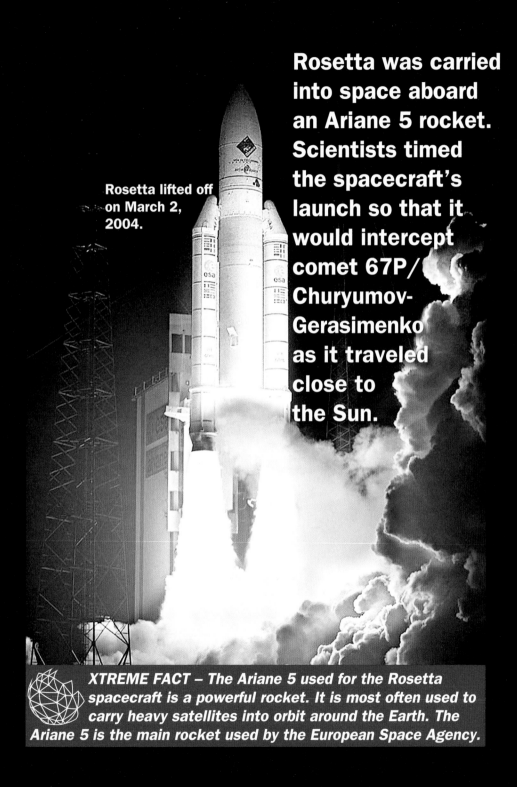

Rosetta lifted off on March 2, 2004.

Rosetta was carried into space aboard an Ariane 5 rocket. Scientists timed the spacecraft's launch so that it would intercept comet 67P/Churyumov-Gerasimenko as it traveled close to the Sun.

XTREME FACT – *The Ariane 5 used for the Rosetta spacecraft is a powerful rocket. It is most often used to carry heavy satellites into orbit around the Earth. The Ariane 5 is the main rocket used by the European Space Agency.*

THE LONG JOURNEY

Rosetta's trip to comet 67P/Churyumov-Gerasimenko took more than 10 years. The spacecraft needed much energy to reach the comet. It gained speed by "slingshotting" around Earth three times, taking advantage of the planet's gravity. It also picked up more speed by slingshotting once around Mars.

Rosetta's Journey

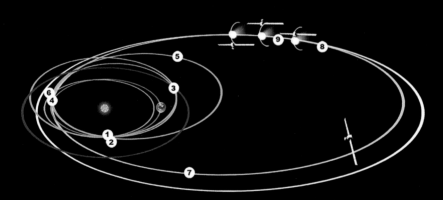

1. Launch – March 2, 2004
2. First Earth Swingby – March 3, 2005
3. Mars Swingby – February 26, 2007
4. Second Earth Swingby – November 14, 2007
5. Asteroid Steins Flyby

6. Third Earth Flyby – November 11, 2009
7. Asteroid Lutetia Flyby
8. Arrives at the Comet in 2014
9. Rosetta Studies
   Comet 67P/Churyumov-Gerasimenko

● Mars' Orbit ● Earth's Orbit ● Rosetta's Orbit ● Comet Orbit

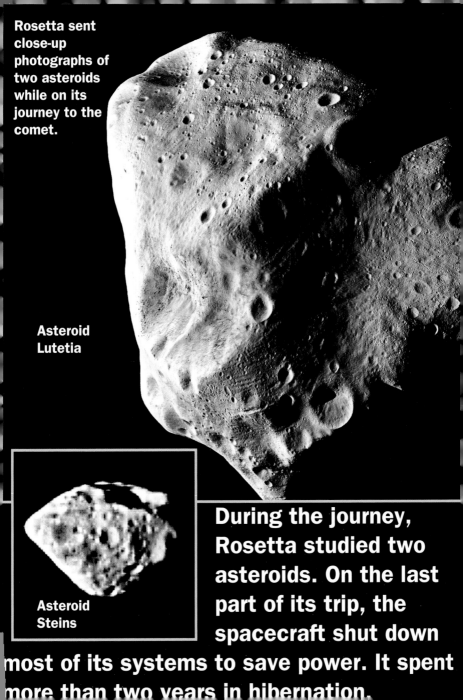

Rosetta sent close-up photographs of two asteroids while on its journey to the comet.

Asteroid Lutetia

Asteroid Steins

During the journey, Rosetta studied two asteroids. On the last part of its trip, the spacecraft shut down most of its systems to save power. It spent more than two years in hibernation.

ARRIVAL

In January 2014, Rosetta woke up. Scientists on Earth were relieved that all the spacecraft's systems were working. A few months later, comet 67P/Churyumov-Gerasimenko could be seen in the distance.

European Space Agency team members cheer after Rosetta "wakes up" and sends its first signal back to Earth on January 20, 2014.

 XTREME FACT – Comet 67P/Churyumov-Gerasimenko's shape turned out to be much more complex than expected. Scientists guess that billions of years ago, two comets collided and fused together, which resulted in 67P's bizarre shape.

Rosetta performed several complicated maneuvers. Its speed had to match the comet's or the spacecraft would fly past. Finally, in August 2014, Rosetta arrived.

Rosetta takes a "selfie" with comet 67P/ Churyumov-Gerasimenko on September 7, 2014.

Rosetta became the first spacecraft to orbit a comet. As it passed overhead, it took detailed images of craters, cliffs, and large boulders. It also sampled dust and gas swirling around the comet. It sent the data back to Earth using its large antenna.

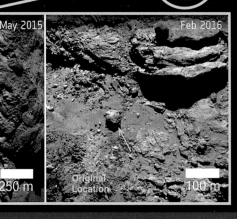

May 2015

Feb 2016

250 m

Original Location

100 m

In less than a year, a 100-foot (30-m) -wide boulder moved 460 feet (140 m) on comet 67P.

XTREME FACT – *A comet's core is called the nucleus. It is a collection of dust, ice, and rock. The coma is a thin atmosphere surrounding the comet. Comas are formed by gasses and dust released when the comet absorbs energy from the Sun. Streams of dust and gas form the comet's long tail.*

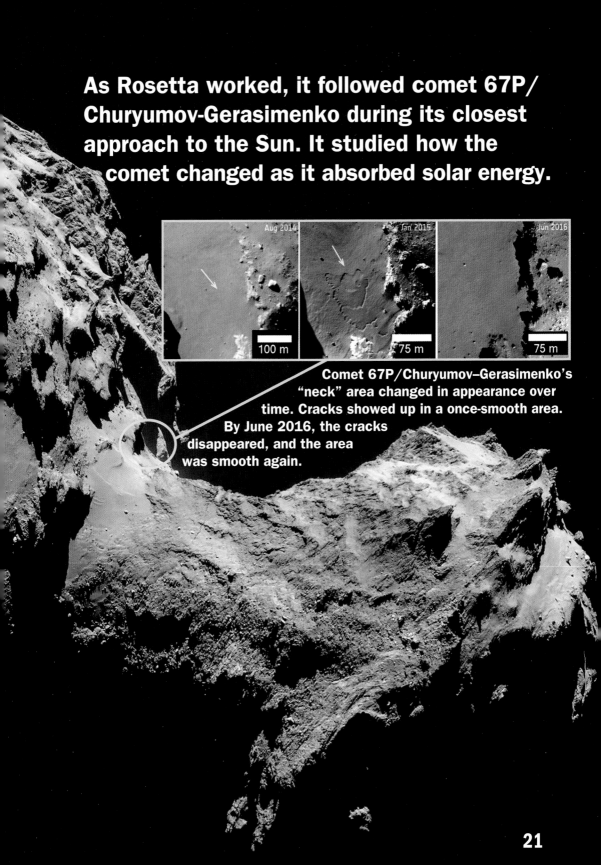

As Rosetta worked, it followed comet 67P/ Churyumov-Gerasimenko during its closest approach to the Sun. It studied how the comet changed as it absorbed solar energy.

Aug 2014 · Jan 2015 · Jun 2016

100 m · 75 m · 75 m

Comet 67P/Churyumov–Gerasimenko's "neck" area changed in appearance over time. Cracks showed up in a once-smooth area. By June 2016, the cracks disappeared, and the area was smooth again.

PHILAE LANDS

On November 12, 2014, Philae detached from Rosetta. The probe slowly made its way down to 67P/Churyumov-Gerasimenko. The comet has very little gravity, so Philae bounced back up. The lander had harpoons designed to hold it in place, but they failed to fire.

XTREME FACT – Philae weighed 220 pounds (100 kg). It was shaped like a square box, measuring approximately 3.3 feet (1 m) wide. It carried 10 scientific instruments, including a camera and gas analyzer.

Rosetta

Philae

Philae almost drifted back into space, but it eventually settled back down after bouncing twice. It became the first probe in history to make a controlled landing on a comet.

Philae came to rest in the shade of a crevice. Its solar panels could not produce enough electricity. Its main battery drained after about 60 hours. But in that short time, Philae was able to perform many science experiments.

One of the first photos taken after Philae landed safely on the surface of comet 67P/Churyumov-Gerasimenko.

Philae sent its data by radio to Rosetta, circling high above. Rosetta then relayed the information to Earth. When its battery ran out of power, Philae went into hibernation.

Philae was found and photographed by Rosetta on April 16, 2015. The lander's square body and two of its three legs can be seen in the image.

XTREME FACT – Between June 13 and July 9, 2015, Philae briefly made contact with Earth again several times. Its battery was partially recharged as comet 67P came closer to the Sun. After July 9, Philae was never heard from again.

DISCOVERIES

Rosetta sent back much information about comet 67P/Churyumov-Gerasimenko. Scientists will be studying it for many years to come. The comet is about 2.5 miles (4 km) across and weighs about 1.1 billion tons (1 billion metric tons).

A false-color image shows blueish tones that may be frozen water ice at or just below the comet's dusty surface.

XTREME FACT – 67P/Churyumov-Gerasimenko is made of some kind of material that is so light it would float on water.

Rosetta discovered that the water vapor streaming off the comet is a different "flavor" than Earth ocean water. Perhaps Earth's water did not come from comets after all. However, Rosetta did find many chemicals necessary for life to form. Did comets bring these chemical building blocks of life to Earth billions of years ago?

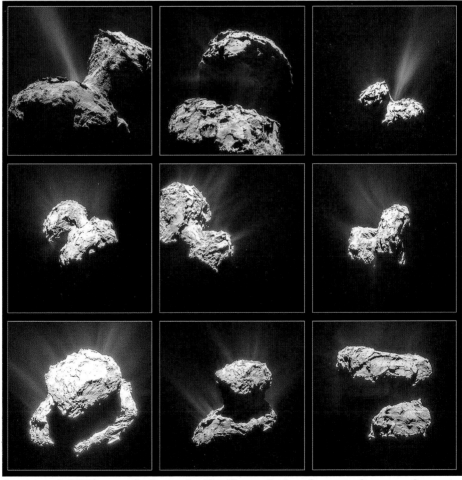

As comet 67P moved closer to the Sun, photos from various angles show escaping gas, dust, and water vapor.

MISSION'S END

As Rosetta followed comet 67P/ Churyumov-Gerasimenko, it traveled farther and farther away from the Sun. Its solar panels became less effective. It would eventually lose power and communications with Earth.

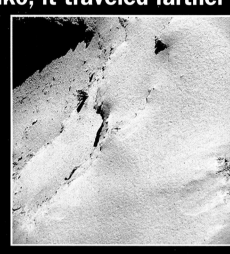

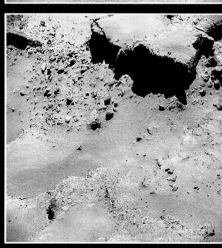

The above photos are three of the closest landscape images taken of comet 67P/Churyumov-Gerasimenko as Rosetta moved closer to the comet's surface in September 2016.

It was decided to guide the spacecraft down to the surface of the comet for one last mission. As it slowly descended, Rosetta gathered data and took very detailed photos of the comet's surface. It landed on September 30, 2016, ending its amazing mission forever.

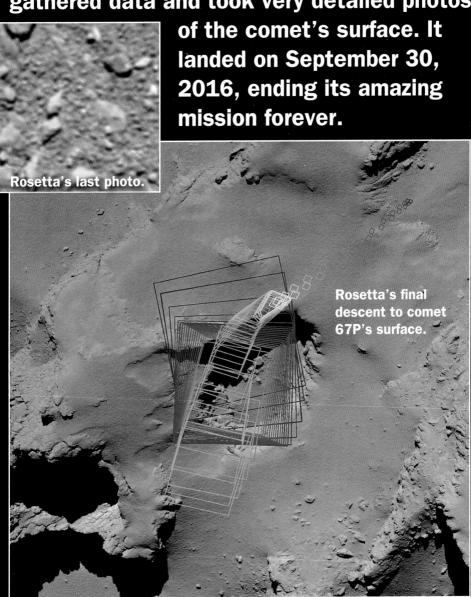

Rosetta's last photo.

Rosetta's final descent to comet 67P's surface.

GLOSSARY

ELLIPTICAL

Something that has the shape of an ellipse, like an elliptical orbit. An ellipse is like a circle that is stretched out. Comets have elliptical orbits.

EUROPEAN SPACE AGENCY (ESA)

A space agency, like NASA, that builds and flies spacecraft that explore the solar system. Its headquarters is in Paris, France. As of 2017, there are 22 countries that are members of the ESA.

KUIPER BELT

The Kuiper belt is a part of the solar system that starts just beyond the orbit of the planet Neptune and extends billions of miles outward. It looks like a large, donut-shaped disk, with the Sun in the center. It is filled with objects such as comets, asteroids, and dwarf planets, including Pluto.

NATIONAL AERONAUTICS AND SPACE ADMINISTRATION (NASA)

A United States government space agency started in 1958. NASA's goals include space exploration, as well as increasing people's understanding of Earth, our solar system, and the universe.

Oort Cloud

The Oort Cloud is part of the solar system. It contains billions of icy objects such as comets. The Oort Cloud surrounds the solar system like a huge, hollow ball. Some astronomers estimate that its outer edge is 18 trillion miles (29 trillion km) from the Sun.

Orbit

The circular path a moon or spacecraft makes when traveling around a planet or other large celestial body. There are several satellites that orbit Mars, including NASA's Mars Reconnaissance Orbiter and the European Space Agency's ExoMars Trace Gas Orbiter.

Solar Array

A solar array is simply several solar panels connected together. Solar panels, in turn, contain many solar cells. Solar cells absorb energy from the Sun and turn it into electricity. Large solar arrays may contain thousands of solar cells. Rosetta was powered by two solar arrays, mounted on each side of the spacecraft. Each array contained five solar panels.

Time Capsule

A container filled with items from current time that is sealed and left to be opened at some future date.

INDEX

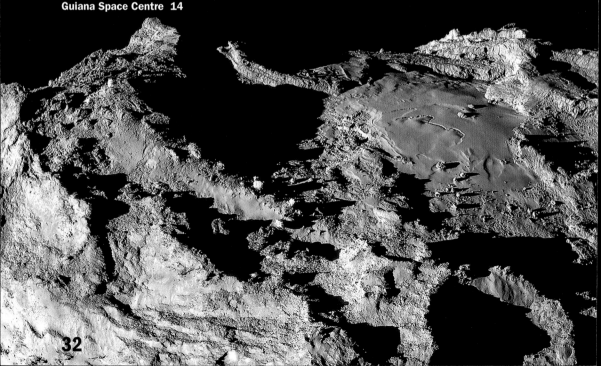